SECURING THE DIGITAL FRONTIER

A HANDBOOK FOR CYBERCRIME RESPONSE

PROF.(DR) PANKAJ KUMAR MISHRA

Dedicated to the brave police officers who stand at the

frontline of justice, safeguarding our digital world...

Contents

Foreword   vii

Preface   ix

Acknowledgements   xi

Prologue   xiii

1. Initial Response   1

2. Lodging The FIR   5

3. Legal Framework   10

4. Investigation Process   15

5. Coordination With Other Agencies   19

6. Common Cyber Crimes   24

7. Preventive Measures   29

8. Resources And References   34

Foreword

In today's rapidly evolving digital landscape, the advancements in technology offer unprecedented opportunities. However, they also present complex challenges, particularly in the realm of cybersecurity. With cybercrimes growing more sophisticated and pervasive, the need for effective measures to secure our digital frontiers has never been more pressing.

Securing the Digital Frontier: A Handbook for Cybercrime Response is crafted as an essential resource for police officers and law enforcement professionals, equipping them with the knowledge, tools, and strategies needed to counter cybercriminal activities effectively. This manual provides actionable insights into the prevention, investigation, and response to cybercrimes. It is specifically designed to offer law enforcement a comprehensive understanding of the dynamic and evolving nature of cyber threats.

The book covers a range of critical topics, from identifying common cybercrime tactics to deploying advanced investigative techniques, empowering officers with the skills required to stay ahead of cybercriminals. As cyber threats continue to escalate, a proactive, well-informed approach is essential to safeguarding our digital ecosystems. This handbook aims to bridge the gap between evolving cyber threats and law enforcement readiness, contributing to a more resilient and secure digital environment for all.

Mukesh Gupta
Chancellor, Future University

Preface

The rapid growth of technology has reshaped our world in ways once unimaginable. As we continue to innovate and embrace the vast potential of the digital era, we also find ourselves facing a new breed of criminal activity—cybercrime. From data breaches to sophisticated hacking schemes, the threats that exist within the digital realm are evolving rapidly, and so too must our ability to confront them.

"Securing the Digital Frontier: A Handbook for Cybercrime Response" has been crafted with the intention of addressing these challenges headon. This handbook is designed specifically for law enforcement officers, providing them with practical tools and insights into the complexities of cybersecurity. As cybercrime becomes more prevalent, the role of police officers in mitigating and investigating these offenses becomes critical. It is our collective responsibility to ensure that these frontline defenders have the knowledge, strategies, and resources to tackle this growing menace.

In preparing this manual, I have drawn upon my experiences in academia, research, and collaboration with cybersecurity experts. This resource combines essential theory with actionable insights, covering key aspects such as digital forensics, cybercrime investigation techniques, threat assessment, and legal frameworks. Whether you are new to the field of cybersecurity or a seasoned professional, this book is structured to provide a comprehensive yet accessible guide.

I would like to extend my gratitude to Future University for its continued support in championing educational initiatives that address the needs of our time. I also wish to acknowledge the law enforcement professionals whose valuable feedback has shaped the contents of this manual. I hope that *"Securing the Digital Frontier"* will become a trusted resource for officers, helping them protect individuals and institutions from cyber threats.

In an age where cybercrime knows no borders, our commitment to cybersecurity must be unwavering. I am confident that through this handbook, police officers will gain the confidence and competence needed to secure our digital landscapes.

Prof. (Dr) Pankaj Kumar Mishra

Acknowledgements

The, "Securing the Digital Frontier: A Handbook for Cybercrime Response," is the product of a collective endeavor, and while I am honored to have authored it, the contributions of many individuals and groups have played an essential role in its creation.

First and foremost, I extend my deepest gratitude to the dedicated police officers and law enforcement professionals whose unwavering commitment to protecting our communities has been a constant source of inspiration throughout this project. Your tireless efforts in safeguarding our digital landscapes are the true foundation of a secure and resilient society. This book is a testament to your dedication and bravery in the face of an increasingly complex and dangerous cyber threat landscape.

I am also profoundly grateful to my esteemed colleagues and collaborators whose expertise, insights, and constructive feedback have been invaluable during the development of this handbook. Your support has been instrumental in shaping its content, ensuring that it serves as a practical, effective resource for law enforcement agencies. The collaborative spirit with which you shared your knowledge has enriched this work, and I am thankful for your time, effort, and dedication.

A heartfelt thank you goes to my family for their unwavering encouragement, understanding, and patience. Their support has been a constant source of strength throughout this journey. Without their belief in my work, this project would not have been possible. Their sacrifices and encouragement provided the foundation for my perseverance, and I am forever grateful for their love and belief in me.

Lastly, I would like to acknowledge the contributions of the countless individuals, organizations, and institutions working tirelessly in the field of cybersecurity. Your pioneering efforts in the prevention, detection, and response to cyber threats continue to shape our understanding of the evolving digital landscape. This handbook is built upon your ongoing work, and it is through your collective contributions that we continue to make strides in securing the digital frontier.

To all those who have supported this project, directly or indirectly, I offer my sincere thanks. Together, we are building a safer, more secure digital world for generations to come.

Prof. (Dr) Pankaj Kumar Mishra

Prologue

In an era where our lives are increasingly intertwined with the digital realm, the threat of cyber crime looms ever larger. The digital frontier, once heralded as the limitless expanse of opportunity and innovation, now presents new challenges that law enforcement must confront. This handbook, "Securing the Digital Frontier: A Handbook for Cybercrime Response," is born out of the urgent need to equip our police officers with the knowledge, tools, and strategies necessary to combat these evolving threats.

Cyber crime knows no boundaries. It penetrates every sector, targets individuals and institutions alike, and evolves with alarming rapidity. Traditional policing methods, while indispensable, are no longer sufficient to address the unique challenges posed by digital malfeasance. Our officers must now be adept at navigating both the physical and virtual worlds, merging conventional wisdom with cutting-edge technology.

This book stands as a tribute to the resilience and adaptability of our law enforcement community. It aims to equip officers with a comprehensive understanding of cyber crime, covering everything from initial response and investigative procedures to legal frameworks and preventive measures. Each chapter is meticulously crafted to offer actionable insights and practical guidance, ensuring that every officer, regardless of their prior experience with cyber crime, can proficiently safeguard our digital spaces.

As we stand at this critical juncture, the collaboration between law enforcement, government agencies, private sector partners, and the community at large becomes more crucial than ever. "Securing the Digital Frontier" is not just a handbook; it is a call to arms, an invitation to join forces in safeguarding our digital future. Together, we can build a resilient and secure digital landscape, one that upholds the values of justice, security, and trust.

Prof. (Dr) Pankaj Kumar Mishra

CHAPTER ONE

Initial Response

The initial response to a cybercrime complaint plays a crucial role in the success of the investigation. In India, where cybercrime is becoming increasingly prevalent, law enforcement must act swiftly and efficiently to collect and secure evidence. Given the digital nature of these crimes, it is essential that the first steps—logging the complaint, interviewing the complainant, gathering evidence, and maintaining clear communication—are carried out with precision. This chapter outlines the steps that law enforcement officers should take immediately upon receiving a cybercrime complaint, ensuring that evidence is preserved and documented in line with Indian legal standards.

Logging the Complaint

When a complainant approaches a police station or reports a cybercrime through the National Cyber Crime Reporting Portal (cybercrime.gov.in), it is crucial to record every relevant detail comprehensively. Officers should begin by gathering the complainant's personal information, including their name, address, contact number, and email ID. It is also necessary to verify the complainant's identity through official documentation, such as their Aadhaar Card, PAN Card, or Voter ID, to ensure the legitimacy of the complaint. Furthermore, any additional online identities, such as social media profiles or usernames relevant to the incident, should be documented. Next, the details of the cybercrime incident must be thoroughly logged. This includes identifying the type of cybercrime, whether it be phishing, identity theft, online harassment, or another offense. The date, time, and digital platforms involved in the crime should also be noted. Officers should ask how the complaint was filed—whether in person, online, or by phone. Lastly, any preliminary evidence provided by the complainant, such as screenshots, emails, or chat logs, should be collected and securely preserved. Complainants should be advised to retain all digital evidence in its original form to avoid tampering and to ensure that it is admissible in future investigations.

Interviewing the Complainant

The next crucial step is to conduct a detailed interview with the complainant. The objective of this interview is to gain a comprehensive understanding of the crime and identify key information that may aid the investigation. Officers should encourage the complainant to provide a clear and detailed account of the incident, covering all interactions that may be relevant to the crime. If the complainant is aware of any prior contact with the suspect, or has noticed any unusual behavior before the incident, this information should also be carefully documented. During the interview, officers should gather details about the complainant's digital footprint. This involves asking how the complainant first became aware of the crime and through which platform, such as email, SMS, or social media, it was conducted. Suspicious communications, including phishing emails, fraudulent messages, or unsolicited calls, should be noted. Officers should also inquire whether the complainant has noticed any behavioral patterns, such as peculiar online activities or unfamiliar login attempts. Understanding the psychological and emotional impact on the complainant is equally important, as it may provide insights into the severity of the crime and the potential need for victim support services.

Gathering Initial Evidence

Securing and preserving digital evidence is a time-sensitive process. Since digital evidence can be easily lost, altered, or destroyed, law enforcement officers must take swift and thorough action to gather all relevant materials. If the crime involves personal devices such as smartphones, computers, or tablets, these devices must be secured immediately and not tampered with until a forensic investigation is conducted. The complainant should be instructed not to use any affected devices until they have received further guidance from the investigators. In addition to securing digital devices, law enforcement officers should focus on preserving all forms of digital communication relevant to the case. Emails, text messages, social media conversations, and other online interactions that may contain evidence of the crime should be collected. The complainant should be asked to forward any suspicious or malicious content they have received, such as phishing links, fraudulent messages, or compromised files. Additionally, officers should ensure that key technical data, such as log files, metadata, and IP addresses, are preserved from the complainant's devices. In more complex cases, it may be necessary to engage cyber forensic experts at the earliest stage. These experts can assist in the proper extraction and preservation of digital evidence, ensuring it is handled in accordance with legal protocols. This is particularly important as mishandled evidence may become inadmissible in court, weakening the case. Forensic specialists can also help analyze data such as time stamps, file integrity, and device logs to build a strong foundation for the investigation.

First Responders' Duties

First responders play a pivotal role in the early stages of a cybercrime investigation. Upon receiving a complaint, the first step is to immediately log it in the official complaint register and document every action taken thereafter. A Complaint Reference Number (CRN) should be provided to the complainant so that they can track the progress of their case. This reference number will also serve as a formal acknowledgment that their complaint has been recorded and will be investigated. Maintaining open and clear communication with the complainant is essential. First responders should inform the complainant about the next steps in the investigation process, including when an FIR will be lodged and any additional evidence that may be required. It is important to manage the complainant's expectations by explaining the timeline of the investigation and providing reassurance about their role moving forward. Officers should also offer guidance on steps the complainant can take to protect their personal information and devices from further attacks or compromise.

CHAPTER TWO

Lodging the FIR

Lodging an FIR (First Information Report) is the formal initiation of a legal process in India and is critical to ensure that a cybercrime case is thoroughly documented and can be pursued effectively. The process for filing the FIR in a cybercrime case must adhere to the relevant laws in India, including the Information Technology Act, 2000 (IT Act), and relevant sections of the Indian Penal Code (IPC). Proper filing ensures that the investigation has a solid foundation and that legal procedures are followed to the letter. This chapter outlines the procedures for filing an FIR, the information required, and the necessary steps to ensure proper documentation and followup actions for cybercrime complaints.

Procedures for Filing

When a cybercrime is reported, the police must follow the correct procedure to ensure that the case is properly documented and that there is enough information for the investigation to proceed. The first step in lodging an FIR is clearly stating the nature of the cybercrime involved.

Whether it is phishing, hacking, identity theft, or online fraud, the officer must accurately classify the type of crime.

The details provided by the complainant should be recorded in a comprehensive format that captures all relevant aspects of the crime, including the digital platforms used and the timeline of the incident.

It is equally important to include the appropriate legal sections when filing an FIR. The police officer should cite the relevant sections of the IT Act, 2000, which specifically deal with cybercrimes, along with pertinent sections of the IPC, such as those related to fraud, cheating, or criminal intimidation. Proper legal classification is necessary to ensure that the case covers all aspects of the crime and can withstand scrutiny in court. Filing the FIR digitally is also becoming more common, particularly in cybercrime cases. Many states in India now allow the filing of e-FIRs through online portals, enabling victims who may not be able to visit a police station in person to report crimes effectively. This method enhances accessibility and convenience, particularly for victims in remote areas.

Information Required

To ensure the FIR is accurate and comprehensive, certain information must be gathered and documented. This begins with the details of the incident itself. Officers should record the date, time, and nature of the cybercrime, ensuring that the complainant provides a detailed account of the events leading up to the crime. Any relevant digital platforms (such as websites, social media, or apps) involved in the crime must be noted, as well as the mode through which the crime was committed.

If the complainant has any information about the suspect, such as their online aliases, IP addresses, or any other identifiable details, this information must be captured in the FIR. In cases where the complainant is unsure of the suspect's identity, any suspicious online behavior, messages, or transactions should still be included, as these details may help investigators track down the perpetrator. Additionally, digital evidence plays a crucial role in cybercrime cases. Screenshots, emails, chat logs, transaction records, or any other digital footprints that the complainant possesses must be collected. Information about the digital devices involved, such as computers, smartphones, or network details, should also be documented to assist in forensic investigations.

Lastly, it is important to record any immediate actions taken by the complainant to mitigate the impact of the crime. This may include changing passwords, reporting the crime to online platforms, or freezing compromised accounts. Police should advise complainants on further protective measures, such as monitoring credit reports or enabling two-factor authentication on affected accounts.

Ensuring Proper Documentation

Proper documentation is crucial for building a strong and legally sound case. The FIR should include a comprehensive narrative of the incident, detailing the events, facts, and actions taken by both the complainant and law enforcement up to that point. This narrative should clearly outline the cybercrime in question, the platforms involved, and the sequence of events. Any digital or physical evidence provided by the complainant should be attached to the FIR, with clear records of the collection process.

If there were any witnesses to the cybercrime or if others were involved in related activities (such as family members or colleagues who noticed suspicious behavior), their statements should be recorded. Witness statements must be signed and dated to ensure their validity and to provide additional support for the case.

Additionally, maintaining the chain of custody for all evidence is critical. In cybercrime cases, where digital evidence can be easily altered, it is essential to document how each piece of evidence was handled from the moment it was collected until its presentation in court. This ensures that the evidence is admissible and that it has not been tampered with, preserving its integrity for the investigation.

Follow-Up Actions

Once the FIR has been lodged, several follow-up actions are necessary to maintain the momentum of the investigation. The first step is to provide the complainant with a copy of the FIR and their complaint reference number. This allows the complainant to follow up on the progress of their case and serves as formal confirmation that their complaint has been registered. Officers should also keep the complainant informed of any major developments or investigative actions, ensuring transparency and maintaining trust throughout the process.

The FIR and any initial evidence collected should then be shared with the cybercrime investigation units or any specialized teams handling digital forensics. Coordination between the filing officers and the investigative team is crucial to ensure that the evidence is properly analyzed, and that the investigation proceeds without delay. Collaboration with cyber forensics experts may be necessary for the deeper analysis of digital data, including

IP tracing, malware examination, or recovery of deleted files.

Finally, all investigative actions taken after the filing of the FIR must be documented carefully. This includes any forensic analysis, interviews conducted, or evidence gathered during the investigation. Thorough documentation at every step of the process will help build a solid case file that can be presented in court, ensuring that the case is handled efficiently and in line with legal requirements.

CHAPTER THREE

Legal Framework

The legal framework for addressing cybercrime in India is primarily governed by the Information Technology Act, 2000 (IT Act), and relevant sections of the Indian Penal Code (IPC). Together, these legal provisions offer a comprehensive approach to dealing with offenses such as data theft, hacking, and the distribution of obscene or harmful material online. It is essential for law enforcement officials, legal practitioners, and investigators to be familiar with these laws to ensure that cybercrime cases are handled properly and that offenders are brought to justice. This chapter explores the key legal provisions under the IT Act, the applicable IPC sections for cybercrimes, and the best practices for evidence collection and preservation in accordance with Indian law.

IT Act, 2000

The Information Technology Act, 2000, serves as the cornerstone of cyber law in India, addressing various crimes related to electronic transactions, data protection, and cybercrimes. It provides specific provisions for different types of offenses, along with penalties that aim to deter criminal activity in cyberspace.

One of the key provisions is Section 65, which deals with tampering with computer source documents. If an individual intentionally conceals, destroys, or alters computer source code used in a computer system or network, they could face up to three years of imprisonment or a fine of up to 2 lakh, or both. This section is especially relevant for cases involving the manipulation of software or system configurations in cyberattacks.

Section 66 outlines computer-related offenses, such as hacking, data theft, and unauthorized access to computer systems. The penalties for such offenses can include imprisonment for up to three years and a fine of up to 5 lakh. Subsections within Section 66 further classify specific offenses like identity theft (66C) and cheating by impersonation using digital means (66D). Additionally, Section 66A, although struck down by the Supreme Court of India, historically dealt with sending offensive messages through communication services. It remains important to know the evolution of cyber law and how subsequent rulings have shaped its application.

Section 67 of the IT Act focuses on offenses related to the publishing or transmission of obscene material in electronic form. A person found guilty of publishing sexually explicit content online can face imprisonment of up to five years and a fine of up to 10 lakh for the first offense. For second or subsequent offenses, the penalty increases to seven years of imprisonment. Special attention is given to crimes involving sexually explicit material involving children (Section 67B), as these attract even stricter legal consequences.

IPC Sections Related to Cybercrime

In addition to the IT Act, several sections of the Indian Penal Code (IPC) also apply to cybercrimes. These provisions cover traditional crimes that have evolved in the digital age, such as cheating, forgery, and fraud, which are now often carried out using computers or the internet.

Section 419 of the IPC deals with cheating by personation, where an individual falsely assumes another person's identity to deceive or defraud someone. This can include online scams where fake identities are used to trick victims into revealing personal information or making payments. The punishment for this offense can be imprisonment for up to three years or a fine, or both.

Section 420 of the IPC is particularly relevant for cybercrime cases involving fraud. It addresses cheating and dishonestly inducing someone to deliver property, such as online scams or fraud involving digital transactions. The penalty for such offenses is imprisonment for up to seven years and a fine, making it a serious crime under Indian law.

Forgery in the digital context is covered under Section 468, which penalizes forgery committed with the intent to cheat. This could include manipulating digital documents or creating fake online identities to defraud others. Similarly, Section 471 punishes individuals who fraudulently or dishonestly use forged documents or electronic records as genuine. Both offenses carry penalties of up to seven years of imprisonment and fines, ensuring that digital forgery is treated as a serious crime in India.

Guidelines for Evidence Collection and Preservation

In cybercrime cases, the proper collection and preservation of digital evidence are critical to ensuring the success of the investigation and subsequent prosecution. Digital evidence is highly perishable and can be easily altered, making it essential to follow strict protocols for its handling.

One of the most important principles in evidence preservation is maintaining the chain of custody. From the moment digital evidence is collected, a detailed record must be kept of every person who handles it. This ensures that the evidence remains untampered with and can be presented in court with full credibility. Each individual who takes possession of the evidence must sign and date the chain of custody log, which should be meticulously maintained.

When dealing with digital evidence, it is essential to avoid making any changes to the original data. Investigators should work with forensic copies of the evidence, leaving the original untouched to ensure its authenticity. Digital evidence should be stored in secure, tamperproof environments, preferably using encrypted storage methods to prevent unauthorized access.

Proper documentation is another crucial aspect of evidence handling. Every step of the evidence collection process should be documented in detail, including how the evidence was collected, who handled it, and what methods were used to secure it. Photographs, diagrams, and written notes can help corroborate the chain of custody and provide additional context for the evidence. This thorough documentation can protect against claims that the evidence was mishandled or altered.

In cybercrime investigations, it is often necessary to engage with forensic experts who specialize in extracting and analyzing digital data. These experts use specialized hardware and software tools to recover deleted files, trace online activities, and analyze complex digital footprints.

Involving forensic experts early in the investigation helps ensure that the evidence is properly handled from the beginning and that no critical information is overlooked. Finally, all evidence collection must comply with the legal guidelines set forth under the IT Act and IPC. This includes ensuring that any methods used to collect digital evidence are legally permissible and that the evidence is admissible in court. Investigators should be familiar with the specific provisions of the IT Act and IPC that govern the admissibility of digital evidence, so that their work is not challenged on legal grounds later in the process.

CHAPTER FOUR

Investigation Process

Cybercrime investigations in India require a structured approach that considers both digital and physical dimensions of the crime scene, aligning closely with national protocols and legal standards. This chapter explains each crucial step in securing the crime scene, collecting evidence, collaborating with experts, and implementing incident response strategies, each tailored for the Indian context.

Securing the Crime Scene (Digital and Physical)

Securing a crime scene in India, especially in cyber investigations, begins with promptly isolating digital devices and preserving all associated physical evidence. This includes disconnecting affected devices from networks to prevent further compromise and securing wireless devices in Faraday bags or similar technology to block external tampering. Ensuring that all physical evidence, such as documents and storage media, is collected and preserved alongside digital devices is also essential, following protocols recommended by the Indian

Computer Emergency Response Team (CERT IN).

To avoid tampering, investigators refrain from powering down digital devices unless absolutely necessary. Instead, forensic tools are used to capture the active state of devices, recording any open applications or visible data. Proper labeling, sealing, and documentation of evidence bags are conducted to maintain the integrity of the evidence chain, a requirement in Indian legal proceedings. Comprehensive documentation of the scene includes photographing and video recording all devices and access points. Detailed logs list all devices and networks involved, along with the names of personnel, to ensure transparency and accountability throughout the investigation process.

Collecting and Analyzing Digital Evidence

The collection and analysis of digital evidence are vital to the success of any cybercrime investigation in India. This process includes creating forensic images of devices to preserve original data, using cryptographic hash functions like MD5 or SHA-1 to verify integrity, and employing writeblockers to prevent any accidental modification of the original data. Forensic imaging ensures that investigators can work with accurate data replicas, meeting judicial standards for admissible evidence.

Data recovery techniques play a significant role in tracing deleted or hidden data. Specialized tools help recover files, browsing histories, and metadata, providing crucial insights into unauthorized access and actions. Analyzing these data sources can establish a timeline of events and support evidence tracing, often leading to the identification of threat actors.

Malware analysis becomes necessary when malicious software is identified on compromised devices. Investigators carefully study the behavior, origin, and potential impact of the malware, documenting all findings to understand how it spread and infiltrated the system. Network forensics further examines traffic logs for unusual patterns and traces IP addresses associated with the attack, using techniques consistent with CERT-IN standards to identify and assess compromised accounts and devices within the network.

Engaging with Cyber Forensics Experts

Cyber forensics experts in India provide essential skills and knowledge to navigate the complexities of cybercrime investigations. Engaging these experts early in the investigation process ensures the use of correct forensic techniques from the outset, maintaining procedural integrity. Establishing clear communication between law enforcement and forensic experts supports cohesive analysis and accelerates reporting.

Experts employ advanced forensic tools and techniques such as memory forensics, reverse engineering, and live system analysis, tailored to meet the needs of the Indian cybersecurity landscape. Their skills in areas like digital traceability and cryptographic analysis ensure that evidence can withstand judicial scrutiny. Forensic experts generate detailed reports that simplify complex technical findings, preparing to testify in court when necessary, making it easier to present accurate, understandable technical explanations.

Incident Response and Mitigation

Incident response and mitigation form the final steps in handling cyber incidents. Effective containment strategies are crucial in limiting an incident's spread, which begins by isolating affected systems to control the breach. Malicious elements are promptly removed, and recovery efforts commence to restore regular operations swiftly.

In the long term, analyzing the breach's root cause enables organizations to fortify defenses, adding security measures like firewalls and multifactor authentication. Initiatives to educate users about cybersecurity awareness further strengthen preventive efforts, aligning with India's national cybersecurity framework.

Thorough documentation of all actions taken throughout the incident response process is necessary for compliance with Indian regulatory bodies. Submitting reports to authorities such as CERT-IN promotes knowledge sharing within India's cybersecurity community, enhancing the country's readiness and resilience in the face of future cyber threats.

CHAPTER FIVE

Coordination with Other Agencies

Coordination with national and international agencies is crucial in managing and investigating cybercrime effectively in India. This chapter outlines the roles and responsibilities of key agencies such as CERTIN, international bodies, state-level agencies, and private sector partnerships, which together support a comprehensive approach to cybercrime prevention and response.

Working With CERT-IN

The Indian Computer Emergency Response Team (CERT-IN) is the primary government agency responsible for addressing cybersecurity threats and incidents within India. Collaborating with CERT-IN not only strengthens investigative efforts but also ensures compliance with national standards in managing cyber threats.

In cases of significant cyber incidents, prompt reporting to CERT-IN is essential. Incident details should be submitted via official channels, helping CERT-IN to track, analyze, and provide a coordinated response to emerging cyber threats. Additionally, CERT-IN offers technical support, guiding law enforcement and private entities in addressing complex cyber incidents. This includes providing expertise on advanced threats, along with recommendations for mitigation strategies.

CERT-IN also facilitates threat intelligence sharing, allowing agencies to stay informed about the latest cyber threats and vulnerabilities. Through threat-sharing platforms, investigators can access real-time intelligence that enhances their understanding of evolving cyber risks. Collaboration with CERT-IN, therefore, builds a proactive defense against cyber threats.

International Cooperation

Cybercrime is often transnational, and thus collaboration with international agencies is essential in tracking cyber criminals and preventing cross-border cyber threats. Interpol, in particular, provides valuable resources for tracking suspects operating across borders. Requests for assistance can be routed through Interpol's established channels, enabling India's law enforcement to pursue suspects with global connections.

Legal procedures such as extradition and international legal assistance also play a vital role in ensuring that suspects are brought to justice in compliance with international law. Extradition requires meticulous adherence to protocols, working with international legal bodies to secure suspects' cooperation and compliance with the Indian judicial system.

Information exchange is furthered by participation in international cyber forums. These platforms enable Indian law enforcement to establish swift, reliable

communication with agencies worldwide. By actively engaging with international forums, India can foster strong networks, which facilitate timely information
sharing and mutual assistance in cybercrime cases.

National Coordination

National-level coordination with agencies across India amplifies the effectiveness of cybercrime investigations. The Cyber Crime Coordination Centre (I4C), under the Ministry of Home Affairs, offers essential resources and centralized support to combat cyber threats. Agencies can participate in joint operations led by I4C, enhancing inter-agency cooperation and knowledge-sharing.

Coordination with state-level cyber crime cells is also fundamental for obtaining regional support and expertise. By collaborating with these local agencies, investigators gain insights into region-specific cyber threats and can access the resources needed for localized investigations. Additionally, working with neighboring states strengthens defenses against regional cybercrime, creating a unified response to interconnected threats.

Private sector collaboration forms another critical aspect of national coordination. By partnering with internet service providers (ISPs) and cybersecurity firms, law enforcement can leverage advanced expertise and technologies that boost investigative capabilities. These partnerships allow access to essential resources that private sector entities possess, such as data analytics and threat detection tools, which are invaluable in tackling complex cyber incidents.

Multi-Agency Task Forces

Multi-agency task forces bring together members from diverse agencies to address cybercrime comprehensively. By forming specialized task forces that include representatives from the police, CERT-IN, private cybersecurity firms, and other relevant bodies, agencies ensure that all perspectives are considered. Task forces operate with defined roles and responsibilities for each member, avoiding overlaps and streamlining the coordination process.

Joint operations conducted by these task forces are instrumental in handling large-scale cyber incidents. By pooling resources and sharing information, task forces enhance the efficiency and impact of each operation, allowing swift action on cyber threats.

Training sessions and simulation drills further reinforce coordination. These exercises foster familiarity with standardized procedures and protocols, equipping agencies to respond cohesively in multi-agency scenarios. Regular drills enhance readiness and ensure that all agencies are well-prepared to tackle real-world incidents.

Public-Private Partnership

Engaging the private sector through public-private partnerships (PPP) enhances cybercrime prevention and response efforts. Information sharing agreements between law enforcement and private companies ensure timely and accurate data exchange on cyber threats, which accelerates response times and aids in comprehensive incident analysis.

Advanced technology and tools provided by private cybersecurity firms can be integrated into investigative processes, enabling more efficient detection, analysis, and tracking of cyber incidents. Utilizing these resources elevates the quality and scope of cyber investigations, allowing law enforcement to adopt state-of-the-art practices.

Public awareness campaigns, conducted in collaboration with private companies, are another vital component of PPPs. Through these campaigns, law enforcement and private firms can educate the public on cybersecurity best practices, teaching individuals and organizations to recognize and report cyber incidents promptly. By raising public awareness, these initiatives help foster a community that is more vigilant against cyber threats, contributing to a safer cyber environment in India.

Common Cyber Crimes

Cybercrime encompasses a wide range of criminal activities that exploit digital technology to target individuals, organizations, and even national security. This chapter discusses common cybercrimes, the methods used to combat them, legal frameworks, and preventive measures, aiming to enhance public awareness and support for victims.

Online Fraud

Online fraud is one of the most frequent forms of cybercrime, where deception is employed to secure financial gain at the expense of unsuspecting individuals. Common types of online fraud include:

1. **Phishing:** involves posing as a trustworthy entity to deceive individuals into sharing sensitive information, like passwords or bank details.
2. **Identity Theft:** occurs when a person's personal information is stolen to commit fraud or criminal activities.
3. **Credit Card Fraud:** entails the unauthorized use of someone's credit card information for purchases, often

without the cardholder's knowledge.

To trace and prosecute fraudsters, various methods are used, such as email tracing, where email headers are analyzed to identify the origin of phishing emails, and IP tracking, which helps locate the fraudster through their IP address. Financial analysis, which involves monitoring transaction patterns, is another critical tool for identifying and tracking fraudulent activity. These investigations are supported by the legal framework provided under sections of the IT Act and the Indian Penal Code (IPC), which specify the procedures for filing complaints and prosecuting offenders.

Identity Theft:

Identity theft is a cybercrime that involves using another person's identity information without their permission, usually for personal or financial gain. Common methods of identity theft include:

1. **Data Breaches** in which hackers access massive amounts of personal data from compromised databases.
2. **Phishing Attacks** designed to trick individuals into revealing personal information through fake communications.
3. **Skimming**, where devices capture credit card data during transactions, is another form of theft often seen at ATMs or retail points.

To mitigate and resolve identity theft incidents, immediate steps are essential, such as advising victims to change their passwords and closely monitor financial accounts. Restoring one's identity often involves rectifying records with financial institutions and regaining control over compromised accounts. Legal avenues are also available, allowing victims to file formal complaints against perpetrators. Preventive measures, like using strong, unique passwords and promoting awareness of phishing and social engineering techniques, can significantly reduce identity theft incidents.

Phishing and other scams

Phishing is a fraudulent activity where deceptive messages are sent to trick individuals into disclosing sensitive information or installing harmful software. Identifying phishing attempts requires vigilance, including being aware of:

1. **Suspicious Emails** that often exhibit poor grammar, urgency, or unfamiliar sender addresses.
2. **Fake Websites** that may use spoofed URLs or lack HTTPS security, indicating a possible scam.

Educating the public is essential to combat phishing. Awareness campaigns that include workshops and informational materials can help people recognize phishing tactics. Best practices include verifying the legitimacy of any request for sensitive information and avoiding sharing such details over email. In cases where phishing occurs, victims should be encouraged to report incidents to authorities and take steps to secure their accounts, such as updating passwords and scanning for malware.

Cyber Bullying and Harassment

Cyber bullying and harassment use digital platforms to intimidate, threaten, or harm individuals, often impacting mental health and well-being. Legal provisions under the IT Act and IPC are available to protect individuals from cyber bullying, and victims can report incidents to law enforcement for legal recourse.

Support for victims of cyber bullying includes access to counseling services to help manage emotional distress. Protective measures such as securing online accounts and blocking harassers can also enhance their safety. To prevent cyber bullying, educational programs should be implemented in schools and communities to raise awareness about its impact. Additionally, promoting digital literacy can help individuals learn to behave safely and respectfully online.

Reporting and Handling of Cyber Crime

Effective reporting and handling of cyber crimes are crucial to ensuring timely justice and preventing future incidents. Various channels are available for reporting cyber crimes:

1. **Police Stations** serve as primary reporting points where individuals can file complaints.
2. **Online Portals** by government and private organizations offer convenient, accessible options for reporting incidents.

The investigation process begins with an initial assessment to determine the type and severity of the crime. Digital and physical evidence collection follows, enabling authorities to build a robust case. Coordination with other agencies and experts is often essential in complex cyber investigations.

Public awareness initiatives play an important role in encouraging people to report cyber crimes and informing them about common cyber threats. Campaigns, workshops, and online resources educate the public about available support services and reporting procedures, empowering individuals and enhancing overall cyber safety.

CHAPTER SEVEN

Preventive Measures

Effective prevention of cybercrime requires a multi-faceted approach, encompassing public education, law enforcement training, collaboration with private entities, and the implementation of cybersecurity policies. This chapter explores various preventive measures to empower the public, equip law enforcement, and strengthen overall cyber defenses.

Educating the Public

Public awareness is a vital defense against cybercrime, as informed individuals are less likely to fall victim to cyber threats. Education initiatives include:

1. **Awareness Campaigns:** Community outreach through workshops, seminars, and webinars targeting groups like students, seniors, and business owners can raise awareness. Media engagement using TV, radio, newspapers, and social media platforms is also essential for reaching a broad audience with information on common threats and security practices. Additionally, distributing informative materials such as brochures, posters, and online resources can reinforce

cybersecurity best practices.

2. **Collaborative Efforts:** Partnering with schools and colleges to integrate cybersecurity education into the curriculum helps instill safe online habits early. In the corporate world, cybersecurity training for employees enhances data protection for both organizations and individuals. Regular public service announcements further inform the public about evolving cyber threats and precautions.

Cyber Hygiene Practices for Law Enforcement

Law enforcement officers must model good cyber hygiene to safeguard sensitive information and serve as examples to the community. Key practices include:

1. **Regular Training:** Providing ongoing training keeps officers updated on emerging cyber threats and effective countermeasures. Simulation drills help officers prepare for actual cyber incidents, enhancing their response readiness.
2. **Secure Communication:** Officers should use encrypted channels for transmitting sensitive information and multi-factor authentication should be mandatory for accessing databases and systems.
3. **Data Protection:** Regularly updating devices and software with security patches minimizes vulnerabilities. Strict access control, allowing only authorized personnel to view sensitive data and monitoring access logs, is also essential for data security.

Regular Training and Updates for Officers

Continual professional development helps law enforcement stay proactive against cybercriminals. This
includes:

1. **Advanced Cyber Crime Training:** Offering specialized courses on digital forensics, cyber investigation techniques, and malware analysis can equip officers with the skills needed to handle complex cases. Encouraging officers to attain recognized cybersecurity certifications further enhances their expertise.
2. **Knowledge Sharing:** Participation in national and international cybersecurity workshops and conferences promotes knowledge exchange and professional networking. Additionally, regular internal training sessions ensure officers stay updated on new methods and information acquired from external events.
3. **Staying Informed:** Subscribing to cybersecurity bulletins and newsletters keeps officers aware of the latest threats. Fostering a research and development culture within the force also encourages innovation and improves cybercrime prevention techniques.

Collabaration with the Private Sector

Partnering with the private sector can significantly enhance cybercrime prevention efforts. Collaboration
with various industries includes:

1. **Partnerships:** Working with technology firms facilitates the development of advanced cybersecurity solutions, while financial institutions can provide insights to prevent cyber fraud and financial crimes.
2. **Information Sharing:** Threat intelligence sharing with private partners ensures law enforcement is aware of emerging threats. Exchanging best practices and success stories further strengthens collective defenses against cyber threats.
3. **Joint Initiatives:** Public-private task forces can effectively address complex cybercrime cases.

Developing community programs with private sector support helps raise cybersecurity awareness and education on a larger scale.

Cybersecurity Policies and Frameworks

A robust cybersecurity policy framework is essential for effective cybercrime prevention and response. Key elements include:

1. **Policy Development:** Establishing comprehensive cybersecurity policies that cover all aspects of crime prevention and response is crucial. Regular policy reviews are necessary to adapt to the ever-evolving cyber threat landscape.
2. **Implementation:** Enforcing cybersecurity policies rigorously within the police force is essential for consistency and accountability. Continuous monitoring and evaluation of these policies help identify areas for improvement, ensuring policies remain relevant and effective.

These preventive measures, when applied cohesively, help create a stronger, more resilient defense against cyber threats, ultimately promoting a safer digital environment.

• 33 •

CHAPTER EIGHT

Resources and References

India's efforts to combat cybercrime are supported by specialized agencies, dedicated resources and ongoing development initiatives. This chapter provides essential contacts, online resources, checklists, training materials etc. that law enforcement officers can use to strengthen cybercrime investigations and stay informed.

Important Contact Numbers

Having key contact numbers readily available can significantly aid in cybercrime response and investigation in India.

- **Local Police Stations:**

  1. Faridpur Police Station: 0341-2670866 or
  2. Write down your nearest police station number
     ....
  3. Uttar Pradesh Cyber Cell: 0522-2390538

- **National Agencies:**

1. CERT-IN (Indian Computer Emergency Response Team): 1800-114-949
2. NCRB (National Crime Records Bureau): 011-2673 5450

- **Hotlines:**

1. Cyber Crime Helpline: 1930
2. Childline (for cyberbullying and exploitation): 1098
3. Emergency Response Support System (ERSS): 112

- **Other Useful Contacts:**

1. Internet Service Providers' Abuse Desks: Contact numbers for major ISPs, including BSNL, Airtel, Jio, etc.
2. Bank Fraud Departments: Fraud department contact details for major banks like SBI, HDFC and ICICI.

Link to online resources

Access to reputable online resources helps officers stay updated on the latest cybercrime prevention techniques and protocols.

- **Government Resources:**

  - Ministry of Home Affairs Cyber Crime Reporting Portal: cybercrime.gov.in
  - National Cyber Security Policy: mha.gov.in

- **Cybersecurity Agencies:**

- CERT-IN: ccrt-in.org.in
- National Critical Information Infrastructure Protection Centre (NCIIPC): nciipc.gov.in

- **Educational Materials:**

  - Internet Crime Complaint Center (IC3): ic3.gov
  - StaySafeOnline (by NCSA): staysafeonline.org

- **Legal Information:**

  - Indian Kanoon: indiankanoon.org
  - Cyber Law University: cyberlawuniversity.com

- **Forensics and Investigation Tools:**

  - Digital Forensics Corp: digitalforensics.com
  - SANS Institute: sans.org

Checklist and Forms

Standardized checklists and forms streamline cybercrime investigations, ensuring consistency and efficiency.

- **FIR Filing Checklist:**

  - Capture accurate details about the complainant and the incident.
  - Attach any initial evidence provided by the complainant.
  - Record initial response actions.

- **Evidence Collection Form:**

  - Document types of evidence (digital/physical) collected.
  - Maintain a chain of custody record with all handlers' signatures.
  - Note observable details and the condition of the evidence.

- **Incident Report Form:**

  - Provide a detailed description of the incident.
  - Include affected systems and compromised data details.
  - Outline steps taken to mitigate the impact and prevent recurrence.

- **Victim Support Form:**

  - Record details of support provided (counseling, guidance).
  - Document follow-up actions or advice given to the victim.
  - Ensure updated contact information for future communication

Trainng and Development Resources

Ongoing training helps law enforcement officers keep up with evolving cybercrime trends and acquire advanced investigation skills.

- **Online Courses and Certifications:**

  - EC-Council (CEH, CHFI): eccouncil.org
  - SANS Institute: sans.org
  - Coursera (Cybersecurity Specializations): coursera.org

- • Workshops and Seminars:

  - National Cyber Security Awareness Month (NCSAM) Events: staysafeonline.org
  - Annual Cyber Crime Conferences: cybercrimeconferences.com

- • Research Papers and Journals:

  - Journal of Cybersecurity: academic.oup.com/cybersecurity
  - IEEE Transactions on Information Forensics and Security: ieee.org

These resources provide valuable assistance for Indian law enforcement personnel, enhancing their capacity to investigate, prevent, and address cybercrime effectively.

www.ingramcontent.com/pod-product-compliance
Lightning Source LLC
Chambersburg PA
CBHW040113150726
48005CB00013B/1682